Our Love Story
How we met – How we live

© Copyright 2019
ISBN 978-1-7329254-6-5

All rights reserved. No part of this book may be reproduced or transmitted in any form or by any means, electronic or mechanical, including photocopying, recording, or by any information storage and retrieval system, without permission in writing from the copyright owner.

Any reproduction without express written consent is subject to fines and legal prosecution to the fullest extent of the law.

Authors:
　　　Dorothy & Isaac Jackson, Jr

Editor:
　　　Rene' Gordon

Poetry:
　　　Rene' Gordon

Publisher:

　　　ReneWritesBooks
　　　www.ReneWritesBooks.com
　　　ReneWritesBooks@gmail.com

Our Love Story

How we met – How we live

Preface

We all love a good love story. There's something about the characters, their struggle, and their triumph that gives us a sense of fulfilment and that warm-heartedness when two people find each other and make it against all odds.

Dorothy and Isaac's love story takes you through a journey of all their days together; from the first day they met, through all the trials and challenges, and on to their celebrations and victories that come with 70 years of marriage. Their southern charm, their love story, and the nuggets of wisdom they share are worth experiencing and reading. You just may learn a thing or two.

I hope you enjoy reading this book as much as I have enjoyed editing and publishing it for them.

You will be blessed from it. I know I was.

~Rene' Gordon

Our Days Together

THE FIRST DAY	3
ABOUT THAT DAY	15
THE BEST DAY	21
MOVING DAY	27
GOOD DAYS	35
BAD DAYS	41
BETTER DAYS	47
DAY AFTER DAY	55

Hello Future

Your eyes tell me my whole life's story.
We met, and it all unfolded with one look. The path was laid out with all the courses known.
I only had to follow my future that lay ahead.
Your hand touched mine, and my heart was captured.
My soul rejoiced, and I was transformed. My future was destined to be intertwined with yours.
You smiled, and I melted into you.
I was yours forever from that first day.
No space or time could keep us apart because we were meant to be.
My life is one with you and you only.
I knew my future at the first look, touch, and smile from you.
I looked into your eyes, and I said hello to my future.

The First Day

It was early spring in April in the late 1920s; 1929 to be exact is when I was born to Mrs. Louida and Mr. Isaac Jackson, Sr. My mother was a native of Columbia County Georgia where she was doing domestic work, and my father was from Edgefield SC. He was employed with the John P. King milling company in Augusta, where he retired after 41 years of service. My mother and father had thirteen children, and I was the eldest.

Dorothy's mother and father lived in Augusta where she was born to Mrs. Nancy and Mr. Fred Patterson in May of the following year, 1930. Her mother did domestic work also, there in Augusta. Her father was a carpenter and painter. She was the seventh child in her family, and she was raised up with three brothers and four sisters.

During that time, we was Living in Augusta GA on Jones St. It ran parallel to the Savannah River. That year in 1929, something happened to the banks on the Savannah River. It overflowed. Everybody had to move from that whole area. The street now is all business.

We moved further over in Augusta to Conklin Lane. That's where seven more siblings and I grew up. I was the eldest of eight boys and four girls. I would do what I could or what was necessary around the house, helping my mother. I would also help to bring up my younger sisters and brothers. We lived in a small house, but we still had enough room to eat and sleep.

A kindergarten, Bethlehem Center, was close by. We went to this school until we was old enough for grade school. We followed the same pattern through grade school. So did Dorothy, although she lived in a different neighborhood. I was a year older than her, not knowing anything about her then.

A family moved in my neighborhood across the street. There was a young boy with them, about my age. We got to know each other and became good friends. We both had bicycles, although my bicycle was a little newer than his. I had just gotten my bike the Christmas past. I was still trying to learn how to balance myself. I couldn't ride as well as he could.

One day, after the schools had closed for the summer, my friend and I was riding around through the neighborhood streets, when we decided to go through another street. We had no problem with cars back then, but we still had to be careful. We were never too far from home, but I didn't know that. I was not supposed to be out in the street on the bicycle anyway. We turned onto a street named Holly Street, not far from home, but I didn't know that at that time. My friend came from Holly Street, so he knew where he was.

As we rode along the curb, I could see about 200 feet or more ahead of me. There was a little girl standing on the sidewalk in front of the gate to her yard. The moment I saw her, I got the strangest feeling in my chest. There was something about her that I never felt before, and as I got closer, my chest started to swell, and my heart started to pump faster and faster. I didn't know what was happening to me or what could have caused it. I felt like I was being drawn toward her. Something was telling me to follow my feelings and listen to my heart. I never felt like that before about any of the other girls that I knew.

We stopped to say hello. She said "hello", but I could hardly speak. She was such a pretty little girl. I finally got up enough nerve to say "hello" and ask her "what is your name?" She said, "my name is Dorothy Patterson". There is something about the name *Dorothy* that fascinates me. I talked to my mom about it some time ago and I told my mom that if I ever get old enough to get a wife, I wish that her first name would be *Dorothy*.

"What is your name?", she asked. I told her, "my name is Isaac Jackson, Jr." She seemed to have questioned my name. "It is a biblical name", I said. I found out later why she seemed to have questioned my name. She shook my hand and asked me, "do you live around here?" I told her, "I don't live too far from here". She had such a friendly smile. I didn't want to leave, but I couldn't stay long either.

She was the prettiest little girl I had ever seen. The way her mother had her dressed made her look even more so. She wore long braids with big white bows on them. She wore little roses like a tiara across her forehead with bangs.

She wore a white blouse with puffed sleeves, red and black striped skirt, white bobby socks, and black and white saddle Oxford shoes. She was the cutest little girl you would ever want to lay your eyes on.

Dorothy:

My father used to buy meal and flour in five-pound bags. The bags were all different colors. When they was empty, my mother would wash the bags and she would give them to my aunt. My aunt knew how to sew real good, and she would make pretty starch dresses out of them all. I mean these dresses were pretty. The teachers and children in school liked them and would ask me, "where did you get those pretty dresses?"

She's the first one of my friend girls to get my attention like she did. I had a lot of girlfriends, but I was not old enough to date any of them because I was only eleven years old; Dorothy was ten years old. Out of all the girls that I did know, ten of them had the same first name Dorothy, believe it or not!

We got acquainted that day, but we had to leave. I didn't want to leave, but I couldn't stay. We shook hands again and she said, "I hope we can meet again someday". I said, "I hope so too". My friend and I left, and I rode home wondering if I would see her again. That same feeling was still in my chest when I got home.

My mom was in the kitchen working, and I went in with her and started washing the dishes. I started telling her about the little girl I had met earlier. I used to talk to her about the type of wife I would like to have if I ever got married and wished her first name would be Dorothy. She told me, "whatever her name is, she should be a good church-going girl with a good personality and attitude".

That's what this little girl was all about. She had all of that and she, at her age to me, was ahead of her time. She acted with an educated attitude. I thought that I may not be the right type of friend that she liked, but she was very friendly. After that, I didn't see her again for about four years. I wanted to go back to where I first met her, but I didn't know her family at that time.

We went to different schools, and that was the reason we had not seen each other before. I asked my friend if he would go back with me, but he would not. It was a long time before I saw her again. Being as many stores that was in both neighborhoods, we should have crossed paths some time or another, but we never did.

Summer after summer went by, and I graduated from the seventh grade from Charles T. Walker Elementary, then I enrolled in Haines High School for my freshman year. Haines is called Laney High School now. Haines was a boarding school for boys and girls founded by Mrs. Lucy Craft-Laney. Boys and girls did not mix. Boys had their section and girls had their section. So where Haines was, Laney has taken its place. I didn't know Dorothy had enrolled into Haines for her freshman year also. One day, a classmate came to me and asked me, "do you have a sister that is in this school?" I told him, "no, but I do have some sisters. They go to other schools". He said, "I'll show you who I'm talking about at recess".

So at recess, he pointed her out to me, and when he did, I immediately recognized her.

She is the same little girl that I didn't get back to see after I met her that summer when I went riding my bicycle. She was just as pretty as she was then. She had grown to be a beautiful teenager. I still had that same feeling about her as I had that first day I saw her. The feeling started all over again.

I told my classmate how I had met her and asked him if he could get a word to her or if he knew anybody who could get a word to her to ask her if she remembered me. I said, "tell her the day the little boy came by her house on a bicycle, his name is Isaac Jackson. If she remembers, tell her to meet me downstairs when we dismiss after school is out."

When I walked out, there she was, standing on the bottom step waiting for me with two of her girlfriends. That day walking her home from school, I carried her books along with mine. I got a chance to learn more about the family. I still had that strong feeling for her. I firmly believe that God is the reason things went the way they did, bringing us together.

Thank God for what He did when we was in the fifth grade.

For the second time, God made it possible for us to meet again…once through a friend the first time, and the second time we met was through a classmate.

After I met her family, I asked her parents would they have any objections to me coming to see her. They said "no, we have no objections". That's when we started dating. Her parents were church-going people, and so was mine. Her father was a Deacon in their church, and Dorothy and I was Ushers in our church, but different churches. So we dared not to be making any mistakes. We ourselves were used to walking the straight and narrow, the chalk line.

You

Seeing you, I see me,
The me that only exists if you are there.
Knowing you is a blessing.
You make everything in my life matter more.
Being with you, I feel whole.
All of me is present.
Loving you fulfills my life.
You are everything I ever wanted.

About that Day

Dorothy wanted to tell me that one day in July around noon time, her sister and she was in the front yard after their morning chores. There was a neighbor who lived across the street from them, a young boy the same age as they were, they called him Spawn. He would wait until they got to the front, then he would show up on his bike and always stand at the gate where she would be, running his mouth.

She said she never talked to him because she never had anything to say to him, until he said to her one day that he was going to get one of his friends to ride with him. She said to him, "you don't have any friends because you got to grow up". So he let her know that he did have a friend. Later on, she thanked God for letting him bring his friend.

Dorothy:

I knew who I could trust as a friend. The neighbor across the street brought his friend by the house one day, and they both were on bicycles. I never met this young man before. That is the first time we met. This young man came up to me on the sidewalk, he asked me what my name was, and I told him my name is Dorothy.

He told me his name is Isaac. I was surprised when he said Isaac. That brought back memories to me. Mrs. Daisy Tutt, the next-door neighbor, used to talk to me about Isaac in the Bible. I wondered how that boy could be Isaac and out here on a bicycle. That night, I went to my mother and told her, Spawn, the neighbor across the street, had brought a young man by the house named Isaac, and could he be the Isaac you all talking about in the Bible? My mother said "no, but if he lived a Christian life, he could be like Isaac in the Bible." My mother said, "remember what I told you all about books and boys? They do not go together. You study your books first, and later in due time, you can think about boys".

I was a young girl and I could see something in that young man, and I knew one day when I got older and understood what boys meant and if I ever saw Isaac again, I can tell him what I think about him. I don't know if he thinks the same about me or not. We just have to wait and see. It was four or five years before we saw each other again, and I'm sure if he see in me what I see in him, then I'm sure God will fix it.

She said she asked God to let me be in her life and later, she said I came back into her life again. So it had to be God bringing us together again.

I'm Here

With every glance made,
With every breath taken,
With every heartbeat pounded,
With every thought pondered,
With every moment shared,
With every challenge overcome,
With every kiss goodnight,
I'm here with you.

The Best Day

In high school, I would walk Dorothy home every day. I had already asked her parents would it be alright, and they told me it would be alright. Soon, we started dating. Later on about the 10th grade, I asked her if she would marry me, and she said she would after we had finished school. It was not long after that we got engaged. I almost missed the Junior and Senior prom because I was trying to get Dorothy to go with me, but she was not a Junior at that time. The prom was for Juniors and Seniors only.

We talked to her mother and father about what we had been planning and explained to them what we wanted to do. They said it was alright if that's what she wanted, so they accepted, providing that we finish school first. Then her father spoke up and asked, "do you see any scars on her?", and I answered, "no, I do not". He said, "Ok. Now if any time you all feel like you can't get along without fighting, bring her back home." I assured him there would not be anything like that because we are too close.

We continued to go to school, and I was going to see her every Sunday, Tuesday, and Thursday.

We continued dating until we graduated. We were engaged when our term in school was up. During that time, we started making plans for our wedding. We made a lot of plans for our wedding.

Dorothy:

I told Isaac, "we can't plan for a big wedding because really and truly, I'm not trying to prove that I love you". It's not the wedding I want, but it's you, and I love you. We may not have much, but with God's help, we will take what we have and put it together with understanding, and look each other in the eye, and say to one another that this is ours." And that's how we live, not "my", but "ours". Satan tried to keep us apart for five years when we were younger, but God fixed it so that we could see each other again.

On Saturdays, or whenever we could get together, we would walk around downtown on Broad Street, checking into furniture stores and actually laying away what we could. Our first furniture came from the Empire Furniture Store.

I had a part-time job while I was in school, and every week, I would go by and make payments on what we had on lay-away. We had a bedroom furniture set before we even got married. When we did get married, we had most of the furniture we needed. We kept on planning for things we wanted to have and the things we wanted to do. A courtship should last long enough so that two lovers can get used to each other's likes and dislikes. Both people should be in a church in good standing.

We had set our wedding date for one year after we graduated. The date and time was September 12th at 6:00 pm, with Rev. H. B. Bady officiating. Now when I asked Dorothy about if she wanted a wedding, she said "I don't know because my parents are not the richest in the world, but we are never hungry, and we are never raggedy". She always says the funniest things, and she was the prettiest thing.

We got under a beautiful arch that was put up in the driveway of Dorothy's parent's house. I will never forget how beautiful it was.

Possibilities and Change

Possibilities surround us at every moment.
At every turn we see change.
Life with you and building our future is
everything I want for us.
If this is the change that will fill our lives,
I welcome it and all the possibilities with open
arms.

Moving Day

When we were trying to branch out on our own, we didn't have our own house then. My wife's family provided us living space until we could get our own. While we was living with her parents, we had our first born. At that time, I was working for Sears Roebuck and Dorothy was a nurse assistant. We needed more room, and we was lucky enough to get an apartment in the Sunset Homes project, where we had our second born.

Then, during that time, my wife's father had a little store in the back yard of their home. He got worried about his daughter, that if she got sick or something, he or her mother couldn't get to her like they wanted to. He asked her if he tore down the little store and put up a little house, would we come and live in it. She told him we would talk it over and see. Finally, we told him we would. He built a little four room house, just right for our little family. Then, our third and fourth children came, so we needed more room still. So we moved to the Gilbert Manor project, while I was still working for Sears Roebuck.

One day, my wife's aunt called her...this was her mother's sister...and told Dorothy if she wanted to, she could move into her house because she was going to live with the other sister. We were lucky enough to have that house for eight years. Our children grew up to school age and was going to school. I had been working for Sears a long time, but I had taken some tests at the post office, and they was giving me a job. This came just in time, because the children was in grade school, and they was about to outgrow the salary I was getting at Sears Roebuck.

We was still living on Milledgeville Rd when I started working for the post office. So after I left from Sears, I had some shares that I built up over the years while I was employed. This helped us a whole lot, getting us started toward buying our own home. At the same time, our children were growing up, almost through grade school and about to enter high school.

We decided to look around for some land. We didn't find any right away that we could decide on because we had to consider the children and where the schools would be located. But we didn't give up. We just kept looking.

One day, we had an idea. My father had relatives living in South Carolina. He had a niece who lived not very far from where we lived. Although we were living in Augusta, Georgia, she was living in Edgefield County about twenty to twenty-five minutes driving time to where we lived. She owned some property, and we decided we would go and ask her about selling us an acre or two. During all this time we was to find a place to settle, our children had grown and gotten further into school.

Dorothy:

When we went to talk to his father's niece about the property, she said to me, "Aww, you don't want to live in South Carolina, do you?" I smiled and said, "try me and see." His father's niece said, "ok, which part do you want?"

We said we would like to have a spot on the front acres. She had it reserved and cut out one-and-a-half acres for us. We had to have the trees removed before we could have the soil tested for building. It took a while to get the trees out, but we finally did.

Everything came out ok, so we got the go-ahead to start building in October 1972.

By December, we was moving into a brand-new house. We had our grand opening two weeks before Christmas, to be exact.

Now, our children have already gone out on their own, and we've been living in the same house ever since. It's been a joyful time living there. Every year at Christmas, we used to decorate to celebrate the anniversary of moving in and to celebrate Christmas. We are celebrating our 70th year anniversary still living in that same house.

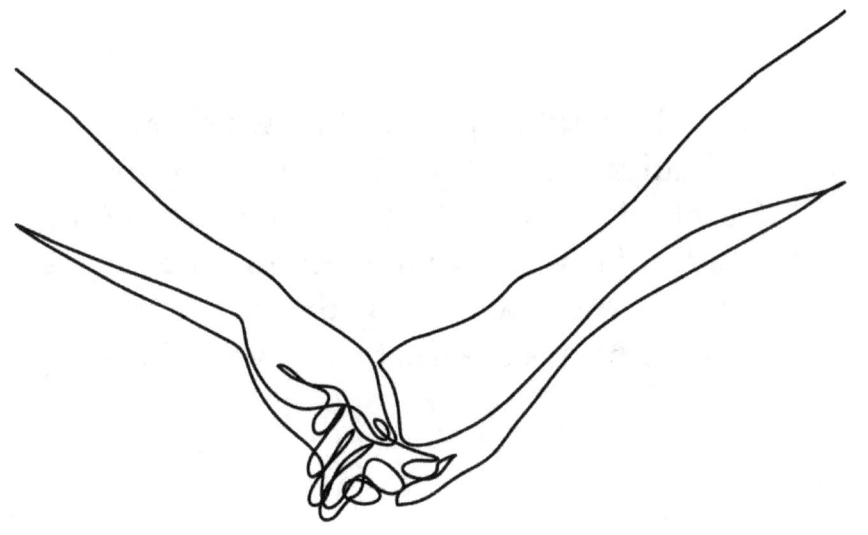

Faithful

Faithful is the love that we share.
Faithful is the hope that we keep close.
Faithful is the time that we spend as a family.
Faithful is what we must be to conquer the world together.
Faithful is the trust we have in God.

Good Days

Everything was beautiful and worked out like we planned. After being married for a year, we became the proud parents of a six-pound baby girl. Two years later came a seven-pound baby boy. About eight years later, we had another little nine-pound baby girl. Ten years later, we had a little six-and-a-half-pound baby boy. That's what we had hoped and planned for...two boys and two girls, and we got just that. We've had a happy marriage. Prayer changes things.

We are a testimony, and we've never been apart or separated for any reason. Sometimes we might have little things that we may disagree on, but we don't fuss and fight over them. Instead, we just sit down and compromise. Teeth and tongue have their differences sometimes, but they depend upon each other to accomplish their goals. As the song says, love is a many splendored thing.

Married couples should be fair and honest with each other. There should not be any secrets between them. A good marriage is based on good communication and good understanding. The vows that are taken during the ceremony should always be remembered.

"What God put together, let no man put asunder". 'Till death do us part, love and marriage go together, and you cannot separate them. You cannot have one without the other.

Keep your vows in mind if you want to have a successful marriage. Trust is another thing the wife and husband should have in each other, and both should be trustworthy. If you can't trust each other, you shouldn't have been married in the first place. There shouldn't be any place either spouse goes that the other can't go. Little things mean a lot, and you should always help each other, especially around the home. As they say, home is where the heart is.

We've been married long enough to have grandchildren, and we enjoy them just like we did our own when they were small. Sometimes, my mind goes back to our childhood days, and I recall how we met the first time. I firmly believe it was an act of God to put us together like He did and led us like He did. He has been guiding us from the start.

Time has passed on and we are proud of our children. They received scholarships at graduation.

Our younger girl, Claudette, received a scholarship in special education and is now a consultant for the Board of Education.

She has also received a Doctor of Education (Ed. D.) from Georgia Southern University. Our younger son, Gregory, received a scholarship in athletics and is now a head basketball coach for Delaware State. All of our children have Master's degrees except our oldest son, Isaac Jr who we call Bubba. He studied a trade in electricity and is now a certified Electrician. Our oldest girl, Janice, graduated from Georgia Military College, Clayton State University, University of Phoenix, Colorado Tech University, and is now with the CDC (Center for Disease Control).

We Stand

Time passes, but we stand still.
We stand strong in our love and our faith.
We stand holding hands, loving and remembering our vows.
We stand powerful, two as one.
We stand, embracing each other through the tests and trials.
We stand together, weathering every storm that comes.

Bad Days

Sometimes life sends you hardships, and God knows we've had our share, but we are a family and we work through them all as a family. We are no strangers to tragedy. Our son Bubba had two boys. One day, we found out that his youngest boy, Cedric, went to be with the Lord. Cedric had the curliest black hair and a smile to warm your heart.

His little laugh was silly and if he laughed, you were going to laugh too. He was just that lovable. His death struck us all really hard, but we knew with God, we would make it through. We know the devil will come to steal, kill, and destroy. This type of thing may make some families fall apart.

Like I said before, when talking about marriage, it is serious and sometimes we have lot of fun and always we have a lot of love. But sometimes there are hard times too, but we stick together and work it out with God and our family.

The devil, being as busy as he is, didn't stop there. Our oldest daughter, Janice, had a daughter name Cynthia, but we called her Cindy.

Cindy was a beautiful and talented young girl and grew to be a beautiful and vibrant young lady. She had three children of her own.

One day, Cindy was in the car with some friends. Someone else was driving the car, and they had a bad accident. Cindy didn't survive. Her mother and three children pulled together to lean on each other. Our family knows how to love and lean on each other during the hard times. And this was another one of the hardest times in our lives.

First one grandchild, and now another. Our hearts were so heavy. Dorothy and I have a strong faith in God and know that God is in everything. So we still stuck by each other's side and didn't let this pull our family apart. It isn't easy, but with love for your family and God in your heart, you can get through anything.

Now wouldn't you know it, that old devil came after our family again. Gregory's oldest son, Greg Jr, had sickle cell. He suffered a might, but his little brother was able to give him his bone marrow and with the favor of the Lord, Greg Jr recovered and is with us still.

He is now a Preacher! What a living testament to God that no matter how hard the devil tried, God came through for us every time.

Our hardships didn't stop there. You would think that old devil would get the hint and leave us alone, but no. I had to have bypass surgery. My beautiful and devoted Dorothy was right there by my side.

She is always by my side. I told you if you see one, you see the other…even if it's in the hospital. If one of us has to be in the hospital, then you best believe the other is right there by their side.

Dorothy is always by my side and I'm always by hers. When she has to go in the hospital, you know I am right there with her too.

This marriage thing is for life, the ups and the downs, the highs and the lows. We are there together working through it all with God on our side.

Sounds of Time

If time has no sound,
then why do I hear your heartbeat with each
minute that passes and I'm not next to you?
If time has no sound,
then why do I hear every tear that falls when
you cry for a love one lost?
If time has no sound,
then why do I hear you whisper 'I love you'
each night before I go to bed?
The sound of time is every heartbeat, every cry,
and every whisper of every moment you are in
my life, and that sound is the sweetest melody
ever created by God.

Better Days

Our family is strong, and we are strong in our faith. Nothing has ever and nothing ever will break us apart. We keep no secrets and we tell no lies. Dorothy is the love of my life. If you see her, you see me. If you see me, you see her. Our struggles, losing two of our grandchildren and almost losing another, none of that kept us from loving each other and being there for our family and each other.

Remember, when talking about marriage, it can be a very successful life, and it can also bring you some really sad hardships, but you have to start off in the right way. Marriage is serious business. It's like two companies making out a contract to do business. You just don't jump into marriage, because this is a lifetime situation.

One thing to remember, never start anything you can't keep up. Like the saying goes, you have gotta accentuate the positive, eliminate the negative, and latch on to the affirmative. Understand those sayings and you can always be on the right track. Do not take anything for granted. Another good saying is, it's not the aptitude but your attitude which will determine your altitude.

If you remember those expressions along with your vows, you will always have a long and happy marriage life.

Marriage is serious. Our advice to everybody at all ages who are planning to get married is make sure you do the right thing. That is, it's the right man or woman you want to spend the rest of your life with. The courtship should be long enough so that each can get used to each other's habits and learn what likes or dislikes he or she has.

Jealousy has no place anywhere. Do not let jealousy get in the way. Be honest with each other. He or she is still your best friend. Even after being married, you are still friends. Communication and understanding are the best things in marriage. So if you are planning to get married, or if you are already married, take your vows seriously. Don't just say them because the preacher asks you to repeat after him. Remember that is an oath, and you are supposed to live by them.

Little things mean a lot. Remember it doesn't have to be all that big to please anyone.

Your marriage can be good or bad, happy or sad, it all depends on how it started. Do not start with anything you can't continue. We have been married for 70 years, and we stick to things that we enjoy doing like singing, going to church, and praying. That's just a few of the things that we enjoy doing. At night when we go to sleep, we are holding hands.

Even after 70 years of marriage, we still feel the way we did when we were young. It all depends on how you feel about your age. You don't have to be old because of your age. Age is just a number so don't think about it. If you think old, you will feel old. Don't let your mind wonder. Keep it occupied with something you like to do. Do some kind of activity that will keep you in good shape, but don't overdo yourself if you feel a little tired. Stop and relax yourself.

Marriage is a serious business, so if you have made up your mind with the right person and you and your bride-to-be know each other well enough, then I would say it's a go-ahead signal. Put God first, and don't be afraid to call on Him. You need Him. He don't need you.

He has been with us ever since the first day we met and been with us every day since then. I firmly believe that He put us together, and we have never been apart, never been separated in any situation. If you see one of us, look closely, you'll see the other one.

I think and feel like we were meant for each other. To teenage boys and girls, or any age who are dating or engaged or planning to get married, we know what it is to be this age and then some. You've got to control your emotions. If you don't control your emotions, chances are you will run into trouble. It could be trouble that you may not be able to handle or can't overcome right away.

Your likes and dislikes are different, that's nature's way. What you may like, you may not be able to have. What you dislike, you dislike. If you really want to enjoy your sex life, plan your marriage with the one you want to live with the rest of your life.

If you are a rolling stone before you get married, it may or may not be as happy as it could be.

Think twice when, or if, you decide to venture into the labyrinth of life. If you want to know something about life, don't be afraid to ask someone who is older and is having a good attitude, like your parents or anybody you can trust and believe in.

Think positive and try to do the right thing the first time. Walk the straight and narrow and you won't have to worry about if you are wrong or not. I wrote this biography along with the help of my wife.

Thinking about it, if and when this book is read, I hope it will help and give somebody some idea about how to get started in life. Not that we did anything any better than anybody else, but it is how we got started and maintained our way in life. Here we are after 70 years. We are still maintaining our way of life in our sand boxes.

A Lifetime of Us

We started as strangers,
not knowing the path ahead.
We became friends,
trusting not in chance but fate.
We vowed to be as one.
Before God we stood.
We fought against all tests,
surmounting them all.
We live to serve God,
being blessed and blessing others.
From the first day to days hereafter,
this lifetime of us is nothing short of God's
wondrous work.
By His hands, we loved, lived, laughed, and let
our hearts be filled with honor and praise for
all of our days.

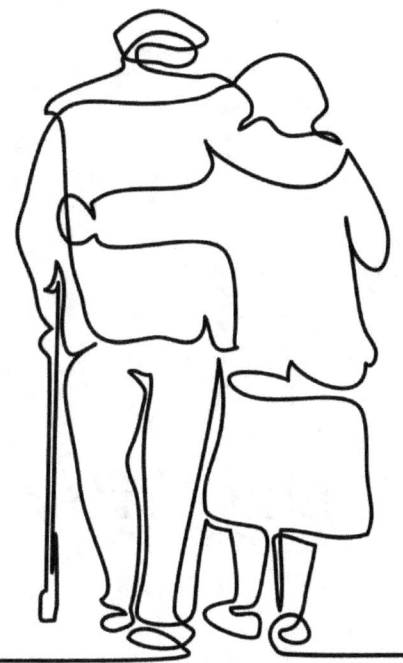

Day After Day

Whatever you do, whenever you decide, put God first in everything because He is the source of everything you will have. Had it not been for Him, you would not be existing right now. Get in a church, whatever your denomination is. Get involved. It has organizations and different activities that you can join. Pay your tithes and contributions as often as you can. You will find that you will be much happier with God on your side.

We do a lot together as a couple, and we like helping others. At one time, my wife and I, after the kids had gotten a little older, we started trying to help other people, carrying them where they had to go. It didn't matter what time of day or night it would be, we would get out and go.

Dorothy always would like to work around elderly people. She also worked with a physical therapist in Meadow Garden Hospital and also worked with two psychiatrist doctors.

Dorothy:

In the hospital where I worked, there were two

men that did not want to communicate with anybody. They would not even go to the dining room to eat together. They would have their food brought to their rooms. Well I was not having that. I took them by the hand and introduced them to one another (as if they didn't already know), and I told them I was taking them to go have dinner and they were going to sit down together. It wasn't easy and we had a little bit of a conversation about it, but they finally went, and they became regular visitors to the dining room together from then on.

My wife was always talking to people and trying to help them see a better way. We was also both members of the Masonic Order. Dorothy was a member with the Eastern Stars. She was the Matron of Chapter #119 (Queen Esther). She was a member of the Heroines of Jericho also. I was a member of the Abraham Lodge, where I became the Junior Warden and also the Patron for Queen Esther Chapter #119. We held those positions until we both got ready to retire from the Order. Queen Esther was rated #1 everywhere they went while Dorothy was the Matron. After she came down from the Order, they really missed her.

Masonry is a nonprofit organization. They went all out to help other people. That is one of the reasons we joined the Order. For over fifty years, we were brother and sister in the Masonic organization. It's a good Order to be in, and it's nationwide.

God was with us every step of the way. So if you haven't tried Him, do it. You will find out what I'm talking about. Nothing fails but a try, so think about it. Whatever you decide to do with your life, good luck.

To everyone young and old, especially the teenagers just coming into adulthood, don't be too anxious to get into trouble. It's easy to get into. Sometimes you never get out. Think positively, take your time, and look into all the angles before you come to a conclusion. It's later after you have already jumped off the building that you find out that you don't have wings, so be careful and live safely.

Like I said before, we are a living testament of God's favor, and if it had not been for God who put us together in the first place, we would not be together today.

We hope you all make the right decisions.

May God bless each and every one of you.

~~ Dorothy and Isaac Jackson, Jr.

www.ingramcontent.com/pod-product-compliance
Lightning Source LLC
Chambersburg PA
CBHW052117070526
44584CB00017B/2531